PATERSON

Paterson: From Garret Mountain, June, 1968

PATERSON

George A. Tice

RUTGERS UNIVERSITY PRESS, *New Brunswick, New Jersey*

Copyright © 1972 by Rutgers University, the State University
of New Jersey.

Library of Congress Catalogue Card Number: 79-163964
ISBN: 0-8135-0711-1 Cloth   ISBN: 0-8135-0719-7 Paper

Printed in the United States of America by The Meriden Gravure
Company, Meriden, Connecticut

To my daughters, Loretta, Lisa, Lynn, and Jennifer

Statement

These photographs of the city of Paterson, New Jersey, came about indirectly from a trip to California which I took in 1965. California is a land of brilliant sunlight; all of it looks newly built. After several months I came home to the East, and the return produced a revelation. The strong light and sharp colors of California had prepared my eye for a fresh look at this older world. Here was time-colored country, almost an ancient civilization, and the atmosphere which enveloped it was predominantly gray. Then, too, it was a world which was everywhere patterned by men, both living and dead. As I looked, I began planning to photograph the obviously dominant expression of the eastern seaboard—the city.

Before beginning Paterson, I photographed Pennsylvania German country life. That experience, a contrast of another kind, strengthened my resolve to photograph a city. Since my project was not a commission, but a personal enterprise, the subject city had to be conveniently near; one that I could photograph at leisure. New York was close enough—only twenty-odd miles from where I live—but I found I could make no personal identification with New York. Even closer at hand there was Newark, where I was born, but perhaps because of that fact, I found the city depressingly beyond redemption. Hoboken, to the east of Newark, seemed to me geographically unsuitable because it presents itself as a fragment, a neighborhood rather than a city.

Finally I selected Paterson. What originally attracted me were its two natural areas, Garret Mountain and the Passaic Falls. Paterson lies in the valley below the mountain, from the top of which the entire panorama of the city can be seen, like a scale model of itself. As I looked out and down from Garret Mountain, I experienced a sense of the city from its creation—how it began, what its past was like, the patterns of its present, and even, perhaps, some suggestion of its future.

The mountain was enduring. It had been there always, an area of rocks, grasses, and trees. The valley, too, was old. It existed long before man came to know it; its river, the Passaic, was then as pure as any mountain stream. The falls, too, had been part of the valley, ages before man and man's city, which their power had brought into being. The thunder of their waters was surely an ancient sound. It seemed to me that if I lived in Paterson I would look to the mountain as a sanctuary, a place of comforting greenness, and hear the falls much as the Indians had done — a voice of elemental power, a source of wonder and awe.

But even from Garret Mountain it is possible to see that the city of Paterson does not match the magnificence of its natural setting. There is a clear deterioration here. Greed and indifference have tarnished the noble promises of the site. I thought of all the people who have passed through Paterson, spending their lives on the way, the diminishing quality of their lives, and I thought also of the people yet to come. Everything I wanted to photograph was spread out before me, waiting to be rediscovered through the camera.

There was familiarity in the detail of the city itself. The streets, with their corner candy stores, their bars-&-grills, their Texas weiner stands, were straight out of my own young days in Newark, though in Newark, Italian hot dogs are more popular. The people, too, were not strangers to the eye. As a boy I had sold paper roses in Paterson; later, I had seen these same people as customers of a New Jersey photographic studio. It had been my assignment to photograph hundreds of them in their homes; the pictures were portraits of children and family groups. The firm I worked for strove for a studio polish in these groups, eliminating the specifics of the particular setting by a portable background screen, which I lugged along to my assignments.

But I did not start my city enterprise with immediacies, the details of time, setting, and people. I began by photographing the rock formations on Garret Mountain, and the corrupted majesty of Passaic Falls. Then, gradually, I began to record the streets and buildings of the Paterson of today. I attempted the impossibility of being at once subjective and objective, so the pictures might serve both as document and interpretation. Of course there is subjectivity here in the final document. Complete objectivity is impossible in any case, and I doubt that it is even desirable.

The use of the bulky 8x10 view camera which I employed for most of the photographs in this volume was time-consuming. I seldom managed to expose more than four or five sheets of film in a single day. On occasion I found myself a minor street attraction; a small crowd of children would gather round and agitate to look under the focusing cloth. Or, with an irrepressible human enthusiasm, they would demand: "Hey! Mister! Take my picture!"

The people on Main Street were photographed with a 35 mm hand camera. As I walked down the street I released the shutter on impulse, hoping to reveal the momentary figurations of the city's people against the timelessness of the mountain and the pattern of the city. And then, at the end of the day, I would return home realizing that photographing a city in this personal fashion —a private project undertaken over a long span of months and even years—is quite different from any usual professional assignment of a week or so. I found also that as the group of Paterson pictures grew, my own ideas were changing. The usual commercial assignment week allows for little more than first impressions. But as I returned to Paterson I began to appreciate the complexity of detail my camera was recording. Dispassionately it revealed both beauty and ugliness, and I began to see that each of those attributes was a function of the other.

I believe, too, that it was good that I did not live in Paterson. That would have been too close to the subject; I would have tended to become a part of it. Vision might have become casual, and when vision does that, you fail to see the significance of the commonplace. Repeated and periodic visits return you to the scene refreshed, vision acute and responsive.

The last time I went back to Paterson I saw a sign in front of a union local hall. It read: THIRTY YEARS AND OUT.

George A. Tice
February 12, 1972

PATERSON

Garret Mountain, March, 1968

Sycamore Tree, December, 1967

Statue of Alexander Hamilton at the Passaic Falls, February, 1968

Garret Mountain, November, 1967

The Passaic Falls, July, 1968

Factories, Spruce & Market Street, September, 1970

Observatory Tower and Lambert's Castle, December, 1968

Christmas Eve, 1968

Factories Along the Passaic River, February, 1968

Rooftops, 21st Avenue & King Street, May, 1969

River Street Railroad Station, September, 1970

Rubel Fuel Oil Company, April, 1969

House at Grand & Dale, January, 1968

Car For Sale, April, 1969

Rock Ledges, Garret Mountain, May, 1967

Main Street, April, 1968

Wrapped Fig Tree, March, 1970

Lakeview Hardware, December, 1969

Moses Market, April, 1971

Jean's Millinery, April, 1971

Paterson: From Garret Mountain, June, 1968

Silk Loom, Perfect Textile Mills, April, 1971

Factories, Van Houten Avenue, June, 1968

The Passaic Falls, December, 1967

School #4 Playground, January, 1968

Backyards, 20th Avenue & Spring Street, December, 1967

Christmas Eve, 1968

Garret Mountain, December, 1967

House on Franklin Street, December, 1967

Christmas Decorations, December, 1969

Cott Beverage Sign, April, 1969

Kitchen, February, 1971

Main Street, April, 1968

Lakeview Grill, September, 1970

House on the Passaic River, December, 1968

Riverside Auto Sales, April, 1971

Chichi's Luncheonette, August, 1969

Tenth Avenue Diner, December, 1970

Garret Mountain, April, 1968

Garret Mountain, July, 1968

Lackawanna Station, February, 1968

Christmas Eve, 1968

Factory Windows, September, 1970

Main Street & 21st Avenue, March, 1970

Backyard, Jackson Street, December, 1970

Joe's Barber Shop, December, 1970

Apartment House, West Broadway, November, 1970

Tree with Carvings, June, 1967

Rock Wall, Garret Mountain, July, 1968

Main Street, April, 1969

Houses, Slater Street, September, 1970

Railroad Overpass, September, 1970

West Street Bridge, February, 1968

Lawrence & River Street, September, 1970

Hamilton Avenue, April, 1971

Factories Along the Passaic River, August, 1969

Joe's Bar & Grill, May, 1969

Houses, Ryle Avenue, March, 1968

Main Street, April, 1968

Painted Peace Symbol, December, 1970

Child's Bedroom, April, 1971

Courthouse, March, 1968

Garret Mountain, April, 1971

The Passaic Falls, April, 1971

Abandoned Kite, Garret Mountain, March, 1970

George A. Tice is an artist with a camera whose work has appeared in numerous magazines and exhibitions across the country. He is represented in the permanent collections of such institutions as the Museum of Modern Art, Metropolitan Museum of Art, The Art Institute of Chicago, and the Bibliotheque Nationale. His photographs also appear in *Fields of Peace: A Pennsylvania German Album* and *Goodbye, River, Goodbye*. A free-lance photographer, Mr. Tice currently lives and works in Colonia, New Jersey.

Paper is S. D. Warren's Lustro Offset Enamel Dull
Printed offset by The Meriden Gravure Company, Meriden, Conn.
Bound by A. Horowitz & Son, Clifton, N. J.
Typography & jacket design by W. V. Cladek